W9-AOJ-860

Nocturne

JANE YOLEN

Nocturne

ILLUSTRATED BY
Anne Hunter

HARCOURT BRACE & COMPANY

San Diego   New York   London

Requests for permission to make copies
of any part of the work should be mailed to:
Permissions Department, Harcourt Brace & Company,
6277 Sea Harbor Drive, Orlando, Florida 32887-6777.

Library of Congress Cataloging-in-Publication Data
Yolen, Jane.
Nocturne/by Jane Yolen; illustrated by Anne Hunter.
p.   cm.
Summary: A parent and child enjoy
the nighttime world together before bedtime.
ISBN 0-15-201458-6
[1. Bedtime—Fiction.   2. Parent and child—Fiction.
3. Night—Fiction.]   I. Hunter, Anne, ill.   II. Title.
PZ7.Y78Nq   1997
[E]—dc20   96-24864

First edition
A C E F D B

Printed in Singapore

For Maddison and her night journeys

——J. Y.

For the book group

——A. H.

In the night,
in the velvet night,
in the brushstroked bluecoat velvet night,

a big moon balloon
floats silent over trees,

and little moons shine through leaves,
through stems, and blossom ends.

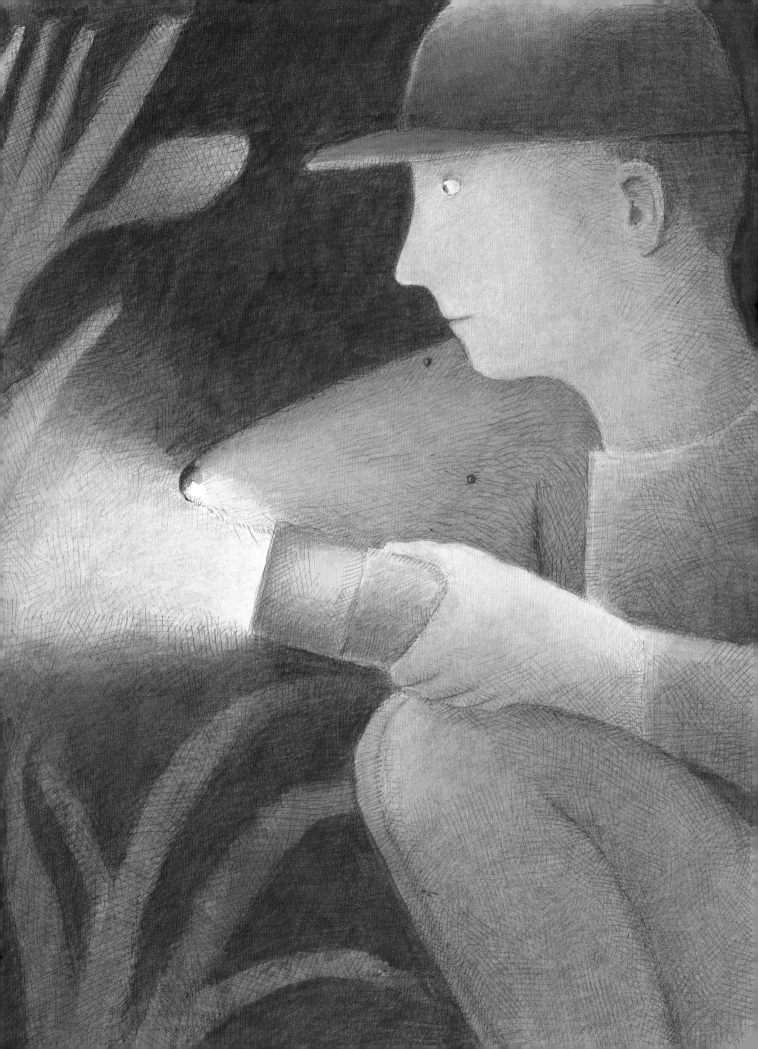

In the night,
in the velvet night,
in the quiltdown quietdown velvet night,

moths flutter up, flutter down,
like wind-up toys, without the noise.

And day is not even a whisper.

In the night,
in the velvet night,
in the wraparound blacksurround velvet night,

a mouse, a mole, a raccoon
creep through sleep,

and owls with deep feathers

write silent passages across the sky.

In the night,
in the velvet night,
in the carpet starlit velvet night,

tucked up under eiderdown
I nestle down, wrestle down
my hullaballooning thoughts

and drift through dark into dreams.

The illustrations in this book were done in pen-and-ink, watercolor,
and colored pencil on 120 lb. hot-press Arches watercolor paper.
The display type is a modification of Chanson d'Amour.
The text type was set in Columbus.
Color separations by Bright Arts, Ltd., Singapore
Printed and bound by Tien Wah Press, Singapore
This book was printed on totally chlorine-free Nymolla Matte Art paper.
Production supervision by Stanley Redfern and Pascha Gerlinger
Designed by Linda Lockowitz